DESERT SURVIVAL
Tips, Tricks, & Skills

Tony Nester

Photos by the Author
Cover photo by Jim Cole

Diamond Creek Press, Flagstaff, Arizona

Published by:
Diamond Creek Press
1931 E. Andes
Flagstaff, AZ
86004
www.desertsurvivalskills.com

Library of Congress Control Number: 2003095158

ISBN 0-9713811-1-9

Cover photo of Monument Valley by Jim Cole, Copyright 2001
www.wildhorizonsphoto.com

Printed by McNaughton & Gunn, Inc., Saline, Michigan

WARNING
The learning and practice of survival skills in both emergency and non-emergency situations can be dangerous. There is no substitute for formal training, experience, and regular practice of survival skills. The author disclaims any liability from any injury that may result from the use, proper or improper, of the information contained in this book. Finally, be aware of any federal and state laws and/or environmental restrictions that apply to the area you reside in when practicing any outdoor skills.

-The Author

Acknowledgments

This book has been an absolute pleasure to work on thanks to the many fine researchers, biologists, and *desert rats* who graciously shared their expertise with me.

Many thanks to my fellow field instructors at Yavapai College who have imparted their knowledge of desert ecology, geology, and natural history. Thanks particularly to Chris Wuehrmann, Bruce Banker, Mike & Joanne Young, Dena Greenwood-Miller, Edessa Carr, Reid Hasler, Bill Walls, and cowboys Mike & Karen Landis. I am especially grateful to naturalist and master guide Randy Miller for sharing his incredible knowledge of all things Southwest and for demonstrating how the land can be a part of who you are.

I am indebted to Dr. Tom Myers for generously sharing his extensive backcountry medical experience, particularly his expertise treating heat-related injuries at the Grand Canyon. Researcher Jude McNally from the Arizona Poison Control Center in Tucson provided valuable information regarding venomous creatures and treatment methods. Randy Babb of Arizona Game and Fish explained the finer points of rattlesnake behavior. Ranger Paul *Crash* Marusich at McDowell Mountain Park relayed, with great wit, his considerable knowledge of desert ecology. Ken Phillips of Grand Canyon National Park Search & Rescue took time out of his busy schedule to discuss his field experiences. Doug Ritter provided data on his fieldwork with signal mirrors and survival gear. My appreciation to bushcraft instructor David Cronenwett for engaging me in many thought-provoking dialogues.

Special thanks to photographer Jim Cole for his friendship, stories, and amazing cover photo. For continually guiding me through the wilderness beyond my keyboard, my gratitude to computer wizard Joe Bodin. Many thanks to Linda Brabant, Dan Mattimiro, and Randy Haas who critiqued the manuscript and focused my thinking into more precise channels.

To my lovely wife Holly who has endured too many days of me being on the trail and then glued to the computer while this book was unfolding. Finally, to my amazing daughter Brooke, who constantly reminds me that the desert, and life itself, is a place of wonder.

Preface

A few years ago, I was teaching a daylong class on desert survival near my home in Flagstaff, Arizona. When we had finished, one of the students came up and asked if he could borrow an outline of the class for a translation project. He was enrolled in the Navajo Language & Studies Program at Northern Arizona University and wanted to use the brochure for an upcoming assignment. Of course, I was intrigued to see the finished piece and he agreed to send me a copy after completion.

When the translated version arrived, I wasn't sure which way was up because Navajo is a very complex language. He said the assignment went smoothly until he came to four words for which there was no translation. It seems that Nature, Wilderness, Outdoors, and Survival don't exist in the Navajo language.

I thought about this for some time and reflected back on many years of working and talking with native peoples. The Navajo, like many native cultures, were not surviving in the desert but living there and they have evolved and refined a complex set of daily living skills that allow them to adapt to such a demanding landscape.

For thousands of years, generations of native children were raised in the desert, playing in the canyons and on the mesas while learning directly from the land. Certainly there were times when food was scarce and life was a challenge but the native cultures of the desert were living and, in some locales, even thriving. By contrast, it's the modern-day hiker, often raised in an urban area, who gets into trouble in the desert and has to survive.

Furthermore, most indigenous peoples were so well adapted to and connected with their surroundings that they didn't separate themselves from the land and, thus didn't rely on words like nature, wilderness, and outdoors. Such words imply a separation from the environment.

It is the mystery of this ancient connection that has long drawn me into the desert. With each trip to the canyons of the Southwest, I learn a little more of the language of this unique place. It is a land that can reach deep inside you and get into your bones. Once hooked, you may never want to live anywhere else.

The desert, however, can be a demanding, even deadly environment to live in. So, if you do have the urge to become a desert-rat, it's necessary to learn some of the basic skills for locating water, finding shade, coping with heat stress, making fire (yes, it can get mighty cold in the desert!), and signaling, to name just a few.

As with learning any new skill, ease yourself into it and practice these skills on your camping trips and hiking excursions. Try to augment your desert know-how with classes in ethnobotany, geology, ecology, navigation, and wilderness first-aid.

Remember the lesson above from the Navajo: that it is possible to become so well adapted to your surroundings that you have what it takes to truly live there, not merely survive. When you finally go to the desert to be a part of it and hike there for a few days or weeks, you may find that this stunning and rugged landscape is a place that keeps calling you back for more. Then, there is no escaping its hold—you are hooked.

Contents

INTRODUCTION

Desert Survival Tips, Tricks, & Skills is the second book in a series of how-to manuals designed to teach the basic skills for helping to prevent and cope with backcountry survival situations. The first book *Practical Survival* focused on the skills that can be used in a variety of environments throughout North America. This book emphasizes the skills pertinent to coping with a survival situation in the desert and how to help prevent such a situation from occurring in the first place.

Like the first book, this one is intended to *cut to the chase* and function as a working manual of field-expedient skills that the reader may find helpful for handling a short-term survival situation (1-3 days typically).

I began leading desert survival treks in 1988 and have been enticed by the Southwest ever since. Over the years, I have lived in, practiced, and taught desert survival in the Mojave, Sonoran, and Great Basin Deserts and currently reside in northern Arizona where I teach such courses full time. The photos and skills that follow were taken from my survival courses in the Southwest but the methods can be applied to arid regions elsewhere.

I have tried to stick to the basic skills that have repeatedly proven themselves effective in field courses. Remember, it is you who are responsible for practicing the skills after having read this book. No amount of reading is ever going to make you proficient in survival techniques. The desert doesn't know you are well versed in survival literature or an experienced hiker and she can be mighty unforgiving if you aren't prepared. Continually practice your skills and soak up as much as you can about this unique land. Then hit the trail and begin your desert sojourn.

There are many sides to the desert, from windswept mountains...

...to rugged canyons on a grand scale.

WHAT IS A DESERT?

To the uninitiated, the word *desert* conjures up images of vast, sandy wastelands devoid of life. Deserts have many different faces though and can include immense mountain ranges, monotonous flatlands, slot-canyons, towering mesas, dunes, and even riparian habitats draped with vines.

The desert, with its openness, mystery, and space can cast a spell and draw you into its beauty. Not everyone is affected by it like this, to some it seems like a place as barren as the moon. With names on the map like Furnace Creek, Hellhole Canyon, and Desolation Point, it's hard to forget that the desert can be a foreboding environment.

The straightforward definition of a desert is that it is a region that receives less than ten inches of precipitation a year. Rainfall and snow melt can vary annually, so some other factors that contribute are: *high winds, an evaporation rate higher than the precipitation rate, intense heat, extreme temperature changes, and a high percentage of solar radiation due to lack of cloud cover.*

There are four major deserts in North America:

1. The Great Basin Desert, blanketed with sagebrush.
2. The Mojave Desert, with its Joshua tree.
3. The Sonoran Desert, dotted with saguaro cacti.
4. The Chihuahuan Desert, with its lechuguilla.

The desert is a land of extremes where you can bake from the intense heat during the day and then be longing for the warmth of a campfire at night. Most visitors think only of heat stress as being a problem but hypothermia is a concern as well. You need to take both into account when traveling during the cooler months of the year.

I was once leading a hike in the rugged inner gorge of the western Grand Canyon. This is a stunning landscape of canyons and mesas on the Hualapai Indian Reservation. We were hiking up Diamond Creek which is a perennial stream that cuts through the Canyon not far from the Colorado River. Due to the heat being in the mid-90s, most of us were soaking our shirts in the nearby creek to aid with cooling.

On our return hike out a few hours later, I noticed some cloud cover rolling in and the wind increasing. The weather report earlier that day had mentioned a low-pressure system moving in but no mention of any precipitation. When we returned to the vehicle, the temperature had dropped considerably and light rain was starting to fall. By the time we drove back to the top of the rim and out of the Canyon, the rain changed to snow and driving was in near whiteout conditions.

That evening and the following day about four inches of snow fell! The highways were temporarily shut down due to the icy driving conditions and motorists were stranded on the roads and in nearby towns.

In the short span of a few hours, we had gone from an environment where heat stress was a concern to one where the potential for hypothermia and frostbite existed!

In the desert, you certainly can't count on the weather being predictable. You have to be prepared for both the heat and the cold.

From the Oven to the Freezer
The record temperature change for Arizona occurred in the city of Yuma. It went from 120 degrees during the day to 39 degrees at night, in a 24-hour period!

PHYSIOLOGY OF HUMANS IN THE DESERT

Humans have always lived in desert regions and have done so through behavioral, technological, and cultural adaptations. Adaptation means becoming like the lizard or the coyote—you don't see them out during the heat of the day. Adaptation also means remembering the importance of the *Siesta*—it's simply too hot and costly for the body to be active in the intense heat of the midday sun. Cultures south of the border know this and invented that afternoon break for a reason.

Technology has enabled humans to live in seemingly barren desert regions through the use of tents and tarps for creating shade, specialized clothing to reduce water loss and protect the body against the harmful effects of the sun, and air-conditioning for our homes and vehicles. Indeed, would Phoenix or Las Vegas exist at all in their current size if it weren't for the invention of the air-conditioner?

Life in arid regions revolves around one key element—that inescapable requirement that no person can avoid or overcome: *the need for Water.* Even the hardiest of desert peoples like the Apache, the Bushman, and the Aborigine can't live without it.

Dehydration

The simple definition of dehydration is a loss of salt (electrolytes) and water from the body. If you're old enough to be reading this book then you have been probably been dehydrated at one time or another in your life. When too much water (sweat) and salt are lost then your body becomes impaired in its ability to handle heat stress and operate at maximum efficiency.

If there's one rule to remember about the desert it's that you can't live long without water. Cut your water intake and your body's ability to handle heat stress is going to suffer, thus reducing the *sand in your hourglass* mighty fast.

I have read different statistics over the years saying that a person can survive anywhere from 4 hours to 4 days without water in a desert environment. I'd have to say that the answer to that statement is Yes!

Yes, because it depends on what time of year it is, your exertion level, how physically fit you are, whether you remain clothed, if you are injured, and if you are in the shade or the sun. As you can see, a lot of variables are involved.

A researcher in Death Valley found that a person sitting in the shade in 90-degree weather over a 24-hour period will burn off 6 quarts of water. So, if you are active the rate could triple to 18 quarts!

Water, water, & water—*don't venture into the desert without it!*

In my desert survival field courses, the minimum water consumption rate is 2 gallons a day per student in the 110-120 degree summer temps of the Sonoran Desert. In such extreme heat, I'd say that survival time *without* water would be limited to around two days, maybe less, depending on the variables mentioned above.

Finally, think of your stomach as a canteen and keep the water in it rather than rationing. You need to be taking in enough fluid so that you are passing clear or light-colored urine. Dark urine is a bad sign that you are dehydrated. The best thing to do when heading out for a day of hiking is to drink 4-6 cups of water in the morning (pre-hydrate) before you leave your house so by the time you hit the trail, you'll be off to a good start.

Don't assume that a water source listed on a map is going to be there either. Some topographic maps were made decades ago and water holes vary from season to season. Plan ahead and carry water with you. This means taking at least 2 gallons per person per day in your vehicle and 2-6 quarts or more if you are dayhiking, depending on the time of year. All of your travel plans, hikes, and scenic drives must take water into account.

Signs of dehydration to watch for:

- Thirst
- Dark Urine
- Headache
- Confusion
- Cottonmouth
- Crabbiness/Irritability
- Muscular Aches & Pain

These symptoms often creep up slowly so watch for them in yourself and others in your group, especially children. A mandatory rest and hydration break every hour is a good way to help reduce heat-stress.

So, How Much Water Does a Person Need?

- Golfer in Phoenix in July: 1/2 gallon during 18 holes.

- Stranded motorist changing a tire in Death Valley in June (on pavement that is 180 degrees): 1 gallon in ninety minutes.

- Hoover Dam worker (during the 1930's): 6 gallons a day.

- Construction worker in Las Vegas in July: 2 to 3 gallons during an 8-hour shift.

- Backpacker with a 60 pound pack in the Grand Canyon in August: 3 to 5 gallons during 8 hours.

One thing is certain, the body must have water. Without it, survival time in the heat could be limited to hours.

Breathe through your nose, rather than your mouth, when hiking. This technique can help reduce water-vapor loss.

Hyponatremia or Water Intoxication

Sodium is necessary for the body to function properly. If you are consuming large quantities of water you can dilute the sodium in your bloodstream or flush it out thus creating an electrolyte imbalance. The result is called *hyponatremia*—a heat-related illness that occurs quite frequently with novice desert hikers and first-time visitors. It is also called water intoxication because the symptoms are similar to those who consume a few too many beers. Slurred speech, disorientation, confusion, nausea, and muscle cramps are often indicative of hyponatremia. Severe hyponatremia is a serious medical emergency requiring immediate attention.

As with most heat-related injuries, prevention is best. For every 30-40 minutes of hiking in the heat, I stop and drink some water *and* have a handful of salty snacks, peanuts, or pretzels. Some powdered electrolyte drinks are better than others so read the label to check for sodium content.

The key to preventing hyponatremia, then, is to simply balance your water intake with some salty snacks. Avoid salt tablets because they are so concentrated that they require copious amounts of water for the kidneys to process and could tax an already stressed body.

One interesting thing I've noticed over the years is the way my body responds after being in extreme heat. Unless I have been living in triple-digit temperatures for a week or more and have become acclimated, I usually go through a recovery period when I return home. After leaving the intense heat, I crave salty foods and guzzle juice for a day or two to help cope with the heat-stress just experienced.

Another *hot topic* has to do with the two ways that the body is affected by heat: 1) Is through the production of metabolic heat caused by physical activity. Holing up in the shade and reducing your energy expenditure can reduce this heat. 2) Is from outside heat from the air, wind, ground, and sun. You need to keep this heat from entering your body and taxing its cooling system.

Cope with these two by employing the following tips:

• Restrict physical activity to the cooler hours.
• Relax in the shade and stay off the hot ground.
• Remain clothed to reduce water loss.
• Keep hydrated (assuming you have water) or conserve your vital sweat (if you don't have water).

Staying Cool & Hydrated = Staying Alive

Substances that can greatly impair your ability to handle heat stress are: caffeine, alcohol, pop, medications such as antihistamines or diuretics, and anti-inflammatory agents like aspirin and ibuprofen. If you use any of these, then you'll need to consume more water to compensate.

Heat-Related Injuries
Connected to dehydration are heat-related injuries like heat exhaustion and heat stroke, categorized as *hyperthermia*.

Heat Cramps
People engaged in strenuous hiking often have a run-in with heat cramps and usually experience them in the legs or abdomen. The problem is caused by sodium deficiency so maintaining an adequate intake of salt along with water while hiking is the preventative method and also the cure. Unlike hyponatremia, heat cramps are not life threatening.

Field remedy for heat cramps:
1. Seek rest in the shade.
2. Replace sodium and drink water.
3. Massage and stretch cramped muscles.
4. Seek medical help if the problem intensifies.

Heat Exhaustion
Like heat cramps, heat exhaustion is usually associated with strenuous activity but can also occur simply from sitting in the extreme heat, as is

often the case with tourists sightseeing and not involved in hiking. Again salt and/or water intake is insufficient.

The symptoms associated with heat exhaustion are pale, clammy skin along with profuse perspiration and rapid, shallow breathing. Other signs include mild confusion, headache, and faintness. Pacing yourself, resting frequently in the shade, and rehydrating along with consuming salty snacks are vital to prevention.

Field remedy for heat exhaustion:
1. Find a cool spot in the shade and relax.
2. To aid with convective cooling, remove as much clothing as possible.
3. Take sips of cool water along with some salty snacks or an electrolyte replacement drink.
4. Recovery may take up to 24 hours so don't push yourself afterwards.
5. Seek medical help if symptoms progress.

Rest, drink water, and be merry.

Heat Stroke

Heat stroke is a true emergency requiring immediate medical attention. The body's core temperature climbs to 105 degrees F or higher and the internal mechanism for cooling is incapable of functioning. Death can occur if immediate steps aren't taken.

The symptoms are the opposite of the above two heat injuries and involve hot, dry (red) skin, along with a rapid pulse and dilated pupils.

Field measures for heat stroke (until medical help arrives or the patient is evacuated):

1. Place victim in the shade and remove clothing.
2. Wet with cool water and fan.
3. Place ice packs or cold compresses on armpits, groin, and neck or use wet clothing to help cool.
4. Maintain an open airway if victim is unconscious.
5. Evacuate to a hospital as soon as possible.

You don't have to be active or exerting yourself to plunge into heatstroke. Just sitting in the sun or on the hot ground can tax your body's cooling mechanism beyond its capabilities. Keep hydrated, observe your salt intake, and rest in the shade frequently.

Once on a hot hike out of the remote Indian village of Supai in the Western Grand Canyon, some friends and I were starting to feel the effects of the 100-degree temperature and our 40-pound backpacks. We had been pacing ourselves and rehydrating continually but the heat and sunlight were intensifying during the last 2 miles of the 10-mile trek.

Nearing a ledge that hung out over the trail, we dropped our packs, removed our shirts, and lay on some of the chilled boulders in the shade for thirty minutes. It felt like a cold, tiled floor and dramatically helped our bodies cope with the heat stress we had been experiencing in our uphill climb.

In the desert, you have to take shade when and where you find it. Don't pass up a shade break when nature gives you one! It might be the only one for miles to come.

Sunburn

All of the cowboys I've spent time with are clothed from head to toe, most even wear leather gloves. The average visitor coming to the desert, though, wants to soak up the sunshine and return home with an enviable tan. That's fine if most of your time is spent lounging by the pool at your hotel. For serious hiking, you'll need skin protection or the damage to your body from sunburn can be severe.

Carry and apply sunscreen frequently to exposed skin. Wear appropriate clothing and a brimmed (3" or wider) hat along with sunglasses. Prevention and preparation once again are critical for avoiding heat-related injuries like sunburn.

Acclimating to the Heat

A friend of mine grew up in Phoenix during the 1950s before the advent of air-conditioning. He said that the heat was something you didn't think twice about. In high school, he took a summer job in a bakery where indoor temperatures hovered around 130 degrees. During his lunch break, he stepped outside for an hour to *cool off* where the temperature was only 110 degrees!

Living with the heat in cities like Phoenix and Las Vegas was just a normal part of the everyday life back then but air-conditioning arrived and instantly revolutionized the means for desert dwellers to adjust to the heat, or did it?

You see, in order to become truly acclimated to the heat, you have to live in it full-time, around the clock. Residents in modern desert cities like Las Vegas or Palm Springs never become truly acclimated to the heat if they are coming and going from an air-conditioned building or their car out into the desert. Thrust into the heat associated with a desert survival situation or breaking down on the highway, keeping cool is a challenge.

Medical findings from Grand Canyon National Park indicate that a person needs five to twelve days of living in the heat before their body is adapted to and begins working at maximum efficiency. This is why tourists dayhiking in the Grand Canyon during the summer often have such difficulty and fall victim to heat-related injuries.

Amazingly, it's often the least-likely people who get into trouble at the park and require medical help: triathletes, marathon runners, and otherwise

Think like a cowboy and keep covered.

superbly fit individuals. They assume that, because of their excellent fitness level, they can run from the rim of the Canyon to the Colorado River and back (an 18 mile round trip) in one day. However, they simply aren't adapted to the extreme heat of the Canyon and exceed their body's cooling capabilities. You are not going to become acclimated and adapt to heat stress during a weekend visit to the Grand Canyon, regardless of your fitness level. *Ease yourself into desert hiking and take it slow, champ, or the heat will get ya.*

Short of living in the heat full time for a week or becoming a baker's apprentice, one method that visitors to desert regions can use is an ingenious method popularized by legendary Grand Canyon hiker Harvey Butchart. Harvey was a mathematics instructor at Northern Arizona University in Flagstaff, Arizona and spent nearly every free weekend hiking in the Canyon. He logged thousands of miles hiking there and knew through experience how to adapt his body to triple-digit heat.

Because Flagstaff is nestled in the mountains at 7000 feet, it's difficult for residents there, as it is with people coming from other states, to become acclimated to the intense heat of the inner Canyon.

Harvey overcame this problem through adaptation and ingenuity. When leaving a water source in the Canyon, he would soak his shirt along with a few extra cotton T-shirts, placing the spares in a garbage bag in his pack. The wet shirt on his body aided greatly with cooling. When the shirt he was wearing dried out, he would simply replace it with another wet T-shirt from his pack. Rotating these shirts throughout the hike enabled him to cope with the heat and helped to overcome his lack of acclimation.

I use this method religiously on all of my summer trips in the desert and have found that a soaking, wet shirt usually dries out in thirty minutes in triple-digit heat! My hiking partners and I will often go a step further during a rest break near water and immerse our entire bodies, clothing and all.

This method isn't recommended for the colder months of the year where it's important to keep your garments dry to prevent hypothermia.

Another tip for dealing with the heat is to place ice-cubes in a Ziploc baggie with holes poked in the bottom. When you start your hike put the bag under your hat and the runoff will help you *keep a cool head.*

In the heart of Western Grand Canyon.

Cotton Clothing in the Desert

In the first book *Practical Survival*, I derided cotton as a fabric that can contribute to hypothermia and be a detriment to your survival. True, cotton is a very poor material for most climates because it fails to insulate when wet and actually robs your body of heat at a rate greater than if you were naked. However, this is what makes it an ideal fabric for hiking in the heat of the desert.

During the hotter months in Arizona where I live, I'll wear a long-sleeve cotton shirt, loose cotton pants, and leather hiking boots. In the event the weather changes, I pack along a fleece sweater and a knit cap.

The Importance of Pacing Yourself in Hot Weather

When hiking in the heat, I usually try and follow a rule of 40/20. For every forty minutes of walking, I will take a mandatory twenty-minute break in the shade to rest and hydrate, regardless of whether my body needs it or not. Occasionally, if it's really hot the rule becomes more like 30/30 or 20/20. Whatever you decide, stick with it so your body has a chance to cool off and recuperate. *Chilling Out* for a while can definitely matter to your body in the long run!

The highest recorded temperature in North America comes from the Mojave Desert in California at 134 degrees F. During the summer of 1996, Death Valley had 40 days with temperatures above 120 degrees. The highest ground temperature at the park was 201 degrees. Summer nights, though, often cool off to 100!

Hypothermia

Despite all of this talk about heat-stress, the number one killer of people in the outdoors is still *hypothermia*. It is the opposite of heat-stress or hyperthermia and involves a drastic reduction of the body's core temperature. As with heat-stress, it can be prevented through awareness. Most cases occur in 50 degree weather so don't think that there has to be snow on the ground. Even in arid regions, you have to guard against it.

During the colder months, carry a fleece layer, coat, and a knit cap in your daypack. The desert is a land of extremes with the cold as well as with the searing heat. Once, on a survival trek I led in the Great Basin desert in February, the temperature plummeted from 20 degrees to -35 degrees in an hour because of an Arctic air mass that moved in!

Also, because there is little cloud cover, the solar radiation that bakes the ground during the day is radiated back up to the sky after sundown. As mentioned earlier, the resulting temperature drop can be dramatic so bring some warm clothes on the trail and stow a blanket along with some food in your car.

As you can see from reading this section, a desert environment places stresses on the body that need to be accounted for. Carrying plenty of water, taking frequent rest breaks to hydrate, consuming salty snacks or electrolyte replacement drinks, and remaining clothed are basic skills for safe travel in the heat. During the colder months carry warm clothes, a hat, and check the weather forecast beforehand.

DESERT HAZARDS

As is clear from the previous discussion on human physiology, the desert can be an unforgiving land for the lost or stranded. Awareness of some of the following hazards and how to avoid them can make your visit to the desert much safer and rewarding.

Flash Floods

Next to dying of thirst, the second greatest danger in the desert is a flash flood. This is the number one weather-related killer of people in the United States. Imagine the following scenario: you are hiking in a canyon where the sun is shining and the sky is blue. There is no evidence of a raindrop in the sky. However, miles up the canyon from where you are hiking, a thundercloud is gathering. Soon, a microburst of rain is going to be pushing van-sized boulders and massive logs your way, driven by a twelve-foot wall of mud. When it comes roaring down the canyon, you will have only seconds to react if you're lucky.

This is what occurred on August 12, 1997 when twelve hikers went into Antelope Canyon in northern Arizona. A rainstorm, miles away, filled the narrow slot canyon with water that reached depths of up to 50 feet. There simply wasn't time to react when the water came roaring down the canyon. Tragically, only one person survived.

Never camp in a drainage during the rainy season.

Research indicates that flash floods generally occur between noon and 8 PM during the height of the rainy season, which runs from July to September. Flash floods can, however, occur at any time of year so keep an eye out for changing weather conditions and postpone your hike for a day or more if the weather looks risky.

Awareness and planning are essential if you are going to be hiking or driving during the rainy season in the desert. Check the weather forecast, plan on starting early in the day, and don't rely just on the sky above your head as an indicator of the weather. Flash floods don't give a lot of warning and can be deadly.

Hikers aren't the only ones at risk. Each summer, dozens of drivers in Phoenix get swept away after trying to cross drainages clearly marked as flash flood zones. According to the Arizona Department of Transportation, nearly half of all flash flood fatalities are auto-related, with about 75% of the fatalities occurring at night. If the road ahead is flooded, turn around and go another way or wait for the water to subside.

Scorpions, Killer Bees, and Rattlesnakes

The first golden rule of desert living is: *Don't put your hands where you can't see!* Remembering this can prevent a lot of mishaps with venomous creatures. This is especially important for children whose curiosity often leads them to pick up everything on the ground. Before collecting firewood, wear gloves or at least tap the woodpile with a stick.

The second golden rule is: *vigorously slam your boots on the ground and shake clothes before you put them on.* Insects and scorpions like the damp, cool climate offered by sweaty boots and shirts. On a camping trip once, a friend of mine was stung by a scorpion multiple times on the armpit after she put on a sweater that had been hanging in a tree to dry. A thorough shake and inspection can help prevent an unpleasant encounter.

There are over 40 species of scorpions found in the Southwest and out of those one can be deadly. *Centruroides sculpturatus* (also known as *centruroides exilicauda*) or the bark scorpion has a sting that can be life threatening to children, the elderly, or those with existing medical conditions.

According to the Arizona Poison Control Center, ninety percent of scorpion stings occur at night in the home. Most people who are stung by a scorpion administer first-aid themselves by placing an ice pack over the bite, taking ibuprofen, and resting. The pain can last for hours or days and there can occasionally be serious side effects. In Arizona, there have been four deaths from scorpion sting since the 1960's.

Killer Bees

What people call *Killer Bees* are actually Africanized bees. They are very aggressive, territorial, and require little provocation to attack. Most desert newcomers worry about scorpions and rattlesnakes but bees should be your greatest concern when hiking due to the danger of anaphylactic shock and the sheer number of times you may be stung if attacked by a swarm. If you hear humming or see a basketball-sized nest beside the trail, head the other way. If attacked, cover your head with your shirt and run to your car or the nearest building. If you have a history of allergic reaction to bee stings, you may want to ask your doctor about getting a prescription for an Epi-Pen to carry with you on the trail.

Some solutions for coping with insect life when camping in the desert: sleep in a hammock, sprinkle cold ashes from the campfire in a circle around your sleeping area, sleep in a tent, sleep on a cot with the legs suspended in coffee cans containing oil (for drowning any climbing insects), stay at home.

Rattlesnakes

On nearly every summer backpacking trip I've done in the Southwest, I have encountered a rattlesnake. Aside from simply keeping your eyes open, a walking stick is certainly a great help for prodding ahead as you hike.

Having spoken with herpetologists regarding rattlesnakes, I found an interesting pattern associated with venomous snakebites. Most victims are male, 18-35 years of age, and intoxicated! In other words, the snakes were provoked.

Admire snakes from afar and give them plenty of space. Be especially aware when collecting firewood and walking the trails during the cooler hours of the day. If you've spent any time hiking in the desert, you have probably walked by a rattler or two without even knowing it. They aren't interested in humans unless you pose a threat.

First-Aid for Rattlesnake Bites

Most of the physicians I spoke with said the best treatment for snakebites are your car keys: that is, don't delay in getting out of the wilds and to a hospital. The old method of *cutting and sucking* is not favored nor is applying a tourniquet. The latter serves to concentrate the toxins in the surrounding tissue rather than letting it disperse. Snakebite kits were met with negative reviews. Most toxicologists and physicians said they were ineffective. In fact, many of the commercially available snakebite kits have suction devices that can treat bites from snakes only up to 30" long and the majority of rattlesnake bites that occur each year are from snakes over 30". The general consensus in the medical community is to get to the hospital as quickly as possible. The good news is that rattlesnake bites are rarely fatal. According to the Arizona Game & Fish Department, there were 1,912 people bitten in Arizona from 1989 to 1998, and only 4 fatalities.

Cacti and Cholla

It seems like everything in the desert picks, pokes, stabs, or impales. Even the rocks are jagged! It is no wonder some of the native cultures had strict taboos about wandering at night.

In arid lands, plants have evolved spines and other protective features to guard their juicy interior from herbivores like rabbits and deer. If you get too close, you will receive a painful lesson in desert plant ecology. Mind your step and survey the trail ahead frequently.

Cacti and cholla are segmented and break off with the slightest movement of a passing hiker's leg. I've seen cows and coyotes with segments of cholla welded onto their face.

Using a comb is a popular trick for lifting out cacti and cholla spines from one's shoes or your dog's paws. The pliers on a *Leatherman* are also handy. Carry a walking stick and you will have a third leg for greater stability and clearing prickly debris on the trail. To avoid embarrassing and painful encounters when camping, determine the location of your night-time restroom *before* the sun goes down. Otherwise, your rear-end may become a pincushion!

Typical Cholla

Sand Storms

One August afternoon, my wife and I were driving from Phoenix to San Diego for a conference when we were caught in a sand storm howling across the open desert. It became so severe that we pulled off the highway and on to the shoulder. For the next twenty minutes, the world outside the windows was reduced to a swirling blend of debris and dust. When the storm passed, we were surprised to see other cars within arms reach of us!

Due to the fact that there isn't much to break the wind in the desert, sand storms and dust devils can happen unexpectedly. The best thing to do if you are caught in one while driving is to pull off the road and wait it out. If it's a severe storm you may want to get the air filter checked out after your road trip. We discovered our clogged filter greatly impaired the car's performance in the heat for the rest of the trip.

If you're hiking and get caught in a sandstorm, seek shelter at nearby rock outcroppings or, if in the open, sit down with your back to the wind and cover your face, cowboy-style using a bandanna.

Agave or shindagger is another desert plant you'll want to avoid getting intimate with.

ANATOMY OF A SURVIVAL SITUATION

There are two types of survival situations: *Those that can be prevented and those that can't.*

1. Preventable Survival Situations

These are the stories you read about in the paper each year. They happen when a person treks into the outdoors with no travel plan, no gear for the unexpected, and fails to exercise that instrument between their ears. Interestingly, the majority of survival situations that occur in this category are associated with dayhikers out for a short stroll. The result is a harrowing, sometimes fatal, survival episode that lasts for hours or days. Poor planning and preparation are the key problems here.

2. Unplanned Survival Situations

These situations, despite proper preparation, often are beyond the control of the person(s) involved. A plane crash due to malfunction or poor weather, vehicle breakdown or a tire blowout due to faulty manufacturing, environmental-injury caused by a rockslide, lightning, etc.... Neither the veteran nor the novice desert explorer is immune to these unforeseen incidents.

Out of these two types, it is the *Dayhiker Mentality* of number 1 that is of greatest concern because it is an easy trap to fall into. The mechanism for disaster starts when you think:

- *I'm not going far from home. It's a familiar place.*
- *It's a state park near the city- how could I get lost there!*
- *I am an experienced hiker.*
- *My new SUV can handle anything.*
- *I have my cell phone. If there's trouble, I'll call for help.*

Regarding the last point on the list above, I'd venture to guess that cell phones may be the direct cause of more backcountry mishaps than all other pieces of gear combined. This is caused by the *Somebody Will Rescue Me syndrome.* The use of a cell phone in the backcountry, like any piece of high-tech gear, needs to be combined with common sense and good judgment.

Also, in many desert regions they won't pick up a signal, so don't rely on that device as your sole means of support.

Both *Preventable* and *Unplanned* survival situations can be dealt with more effectively by carrying a good survival kit. I'll delve into the specifics of this kit on the next page but first I want to tie this in with what you can do to help prevent one of these unpleasant situations from happening altogether.

The 3 Critical Steps to Take Before Your Hike or Drive:

1. Leave a travel plan with someone.

This is a safety net so that if you don't return home on time a system is in place to begin a search. Your family or friends will know that if you are 2 hours overdue (discuss the timeline with that person before your trip), then they will contact the local authorities. This could mean the difference between spending a life-threatening night in the elements or making it back home a few hours later because someone knew where to send the searchers.

2. Carry some gear in case you do become stranded.

The Kalahari Bushmen in central Africa have lived in the desert for thousands of years and traditionally carried up to 25 pounds of "survival" gear for daily living, so why do we modern outdoor explorers think we can get by with just the clothes on our back when out on a dayhike! Carry a basic survival kit so that you can take care of the *big four* priorities: Shelter, Water, Fire, & Signaling.

My survival kit contains: three firelighting devices, a knife, 50' rope, space blanket, signal mirror, garbage bag (instant shelter and more), iodine tablets for purifying water, mini first-aid kit, salty snacks, and 2-6 quarts of water, depending on the season. Coupled with a brimmed hat, sunscreen, and proper clothing, this is my bare minimum gear.

3. Use that survival kit between your ears!

Common sense and knowing your limits are important in the back-country, whether in the desert, the forest, or the mountains. Many tragedies and mishaps can be averted in the first place by using your brain.

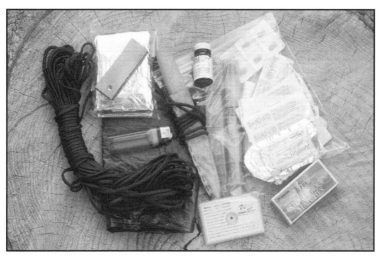

Where do you find the necessities for surviving in the desert? *In your pack because you came prepared.* Don't leave home without the basics.

If you are lost, then sit down, relax, and assess your situation. Then come up with a plan of action for staying alive until help gets to you.

Always implement these three important steps when venturing into the desert and you will be ahead of the game should you encounter Murphy's Law on the trail.

Survival Situations Outside of the Wilderness

Remote desert regions aren't the only place that a survival episode can occur. Each year in my home state of Arizona, stranded motorists on I-17, north of Phoenix, are placed in potentially life-threatening predicaments in the extreme heat when their car overheats or blows a tire. Stranded on the shoulder of the road, they may have to wait for hours in the blistering heat until help arrives or they can repair their vehicle. A person can succumb to heat-stroke in this setting and they're not even in the wilderness!

In many regions of the arid Southwest, there are long stretches of highway between towns so it is essential to be prepared with the proper gear. You don't want your family vacation to turn into a harrowing survival episode. I have driven down desert roads for up to 40 miles without seeing another car all day. In some regions, days could pass before another vehicle drives by. If you break down in such a setting, help might be a long time coming! More on this in the upcoming section on *Outfitting Your Vehicle*.

On road trips, you need to be self-contained with
water & supplies.

THE BASIC SKILLS OF SURVIVAL

Since the majority of survival situations normally last from 24-72 hours, you need to know skills that will take care of the short-term necessities of life. There are seven key areas that you need to take care of in a survival situation. They are:

PMA
Water
Shelter
Fire
Signaling
First-Aid
Sleep

1. PMA

Positive Mental Attitude is critical in everything we attempt in life and you better believe it becomes important in a survival situation where the deck may not be stacked in your favor. Why do some people make it and others don't? Because they persevere and *never* give up, no matter how grim things look. Knowing that you WILL MAKE IT is the mindset you must possess.

Find a reason to make it back alive, whether it's your spouse, kids, personal faith, pet iguana or whatever but make it stick and don't give up.

The first thing to do if you are lost is to sit still, take a deep breath, and remain calm. A calm mind is one that can make decisions and you are going to make plenty of them. Next, assess your situation—*Are you injured? Did you leave a travel plan with someone? How much water do you have? What must you do to survive the day or night ahead?*

Most Search & Rescue personnel recommend staying put— it makes their job easier and prevents you from wandering out of the search radius.

Each survival situation is unique though and there are exceptions. For instance, if you are in a deep slot canyon or ravine where no one can see you, then you might have to move to an open area. If you didn't leave a travel plan and no one knows you are lost then you're on your own. You then have to decide whether to hike out or stay put.

The FEAR Factor

It's easy for me to say that you should relax and be calm if you're lost. The fact is that you are probably going to be afraid—of the unknown, of the nighttime, of discomfort. Having been involved in the outdoors most of my life, there were plenty of times in my youth when I became turned around (we survival instructors never admit to being lost—*only turned around*) and had that uneasy feeling of fear well up inside. The important thing to remember is that it's OK to be afraid.

Fear is the brain's natural reaction to stress and one that has kept our species alive in the wilds for millions of years. You and I wouldn't be here today if it weren't for the fear factor. It will keep you going as long as it doesn't progress into panic. So, sit, breath, and remember that fear will come and go throughout your stay but don't let it get the best of you.

Know You WILL Make It!

2. Water

We humans can't live long without this precious substance. Water is at the top of the list in a desert survival situation and I can't stress enough the importance of bringing plenty with you. Keep it in your stomach, not your canteen and check your urine output: *you want clear fluid.*

3. Shelter

You should never be caught without an *emergency blanket* in your pack and an umbrella in the vehicle. These are basic shelter necessities for creating shade and blocking the wind. A brimmed hat, sunscreen, and sunglasses are also important *shelter* items.

Shelter also includes the clothing you wear which should be loose fitting to allow for air circulation. Style yourself after the cowboys—have you ever seen one wearing shorts, a tank-top, and sandals while atop their horse?

StormProof Matches, lighter, and magnesium spark-rod.

4. Fire

Firemaking is an essential skill for desert hikers to know. If its not needed for warmth then it will be needed for purifying water, cooking, providing light, and signaling. Desert nights in winter can plummet 50 or more degrees after sunset and hypothermia can be a serious concern. Always carrying 3 firemaking implements.

5. Signaling

Unless you want to remain a permanent desert survivor, you'll need to be able to signal so you can expedite your rescue. Nine times out of ten, you are going to stay put and await rescue (assuming you left a travel plan with someone) so knowing how to attract attention to your location is critical.

6. First-Aid

Many survival situations have injury associated with them. Venomous bites, sprained ankles, lightning strikes, rockfalls, and vehicle rollovers are just a few of the environmental accidents that befall desert explorers each year. Carry a good first-aid kit that you are thoroughly familiar with and consider taking a wilderness first-aid course. At the very least, you should know how to recognize the symptoms of dehydration, heat-stress, and hypothermia.

7. Sleep

A true survival situation is physically and mentally grueling. The fatigue experienced can wear even the fittest person down. By taking care of your shelter, water, and fire needs you will be headed in the right direction for getting a night's sleep. Don't overlook the importance of rest-you're going to need it so sleep and catnap when you can!

These seven priorities are essential in any environment not only in the desert. What about food, you say? Because we're looking at the short-term situation, you don't have to worry about foraging for edible plants or snaring kangaroos. If you packed some along then great but it's not essential for survival in the short-term. People have endured 40+ days without food so keep those cravings for pizza and ice cream under control until after your rescue.

Cowboy Survival

While teaching a workshop at a local dude ranch a few years ago, an old cowboy with a face like weathered driftwood, sat down and listened to my talk. In between rolling a cigarette, he would look up from time to time and grin. After finishing my discussion of the seven survival priorities, he stood, lit his smoke, and said, *Young fella there are only three things you need to survive in this here desert: women, whiskey, and a deck of cards!*

OUTFITTING YOUR VEHICLE

Your car or truck is your lifeline back to civilization so it is absolutely essential to thoroughly inspect the vehicle before any excursion. You must also be able to handle basic repairs as help may be a long way off if you break down.

The road less-traveled means you had better be prepared.

You might get away with minor neglect of your vehicle in the city where a quick call on your cell phone can summon a tow truck or friend to bail you out. In the remote regions of the desert, such neglect could be deadly. Make sure you know the basics of changing a tire, and check all the fluid levels before, during, and after a long road trip.

Driving on rutted and rocky roads, maneuvering up hills and washes, and rolling along on blacktop that is 160+ degrees can tax even the best truck or SUV.

In researching this section, I interviewed professional mechanics near Death Valley, Phoenix, and Flagstaff to get their advice and find out what the most common problems are that desert drivers encounter. The top three vehicle problems that these mechanics all agreed on were:

1. Flat tire or blowout due to a worn-out tire or improper tire pressure.

Another preparation issue here: check your tires before you leave home. Look at the tread and scan for any bulges or bald spots. Read your manual and inflate the tires to the proper pressure.

For a puncture, avoid removing objects like a nail or other debris that has pierced the tire since this is holding in the remaining air. If you have a can of Tire Inflator then use it and drive slowly back to the highway. A Safety-Seal tire repair kit is also a handy thing to carry.

Regarding spare tires, carry two if you spend a lot of time off the beaten path and know how to change the spare on your particular vehicle (each one is unique). All of this takes only minutes in front of your house but can help prevent hours or days of being stranded in the desert.

2. The radiator overheats or a hose breaks because it was overdue on replacement.

An overheated radiator is like an overheated body: *it needs to be rested and allowed to cool off.* Don't attempt to unscrew the cap on an overheated radiator or you may end up with third degree burns on your face and arms. Instead, park the car, raise the hood, and then let it cool off before attempting to open it. In extreme heat, you may have to let the radiator cool for several hours before removing the radiator cap and replacing the coolant (hopefully you brought some).

Should a hose leak or rupture, wrap the damaged area with a heavy dose of duct tape being careful of the hot liquid squirting out (duct tape is an explorer's best friend so carry a roll in your trunk).

This is a very primitive setup that may be short-lived but it might, at least, get you a few miles closer to the highway and help.

Afterwards, drive slowly and watch the heat gauge. If it starts to rise, turn the heater on high (which means rolling the windows down too) and pop the hood up an inch to aid in cooling. I used to do this on a regular basis during the steep drive from Phoenix to Flagstaff with my old clunker and its weary radiator.

For desert drivers, radiator hoses should be replaced periodically by a mechanic whether they need it or not. I try to replace mine every two years. The old ones are thrown in the trunk for backup.

3. Overestimating the vehicle's capabilities.

"I can't tell you how many tows I do each week on SUV's, jeeps, and 4x4 trucks because the owner thought his rig was invincible," were the words of one mechanic in Flagstaff, Arizona. "Most people think their truck or SUV can handle anything until they get stuck 18 miles from the highway and realize they have to spend a night out in the heat. Cell phones don't cut it in many areas in the desert so it turns into a serious crisis, especially if kids are along."

Remember that all vehicles, regardless of the hype on TV, still follow the laws of physics and have limitations. Exercise common sense and don't push your vehicle past its limitations.

Obviously there are dozens of other mechanical problems that can occur but these are the top three that most desert travelers encounter and can often be remedied with foresight. Unless you want to risk being stranded in a desert furnace of 120 degrees, CHECK OUT your vehicle before it rolls out of the driveway on your vacation!

Basic Vehicle Gear

- Multi-tool (such as a Leatherman)
- Screwdrivers & crescent wrench
- Duct tape
- Flashlight
- First-aid kit
- Radiator coolant & 2 quarts oil
- Can of Tire Inflator
- Foam pad
- Umbrella & emergency blanket or tarp
- Salty snacks & water- minimum 2 gallons per person, per day
- Brimmed hat, leather gloves, & sunscreen
- Blanket, wool cap, and food (for the winter months)
- Communications- Satellite phone, CB, or Ham Radio
- Vehicle manual & appropriate maps
- A good jack that you have tested!
- A spare tire (or two) that you have inspected!

Depending on your vehicle, the season, and distance being traveled, you may want to carry more gear. I usually have 10 gallons of water in my truck because of the remote regions I venture into. This is in *addition* to the water bottles carried in my pack for dayhikes.

A means of communicating is also essential, especially for solo travelers. The price of Satellite phones is dropping each year and they are very reliable compared to cell phones, which lack coverage in many desert regions.

I know of a geologist who travels alone in isolated areas of Utah and carries enough gear so that he is self-contained. He keeps his jeep stocked with extra gas, a Ham-radio, stove, food, flares, winch, sleeping bag, chains, air compressor, Safety-Seal tire repair kit, and a shovel. At least carry the basics on the list above and you can decide to add more later based on your travel needs.

Experienced travelers enjoying Death Valley.

Water

As already mentioned, you can't live long without water. You also don't have to be in the middle of a remote desert region to succumb to dehydration or heat stroke. Due to the intense heat of summer, a person changing a tire on the highway may be exposed to a ground temperature of 160+ degrees and an air temperature of 110 degrees. Carry at least 2 gallons of water per person, per day. You just can't have too much!

Umbrella

This handy tool isn't for the rain but for creating instant shade when working on your car, waiting for a tow truck, or walking to a gas station. An umbrella is an essential piece of gear and it can provide a shaded spot that is 10-15 degrees cooler than the surrounding area. *Tip— Avoid black.*

Special Considerations for Traveling with Children

Keep in mind that if your car has been sitting in the sun, the metal parts of the seat belt are capable of burning exposed skin so wrap them and cool off the interior sufficiently before placing your child in the seat. If you have to work on the car don't leave your child inside the hot vehicle. Set up a shade shelter nearby for them to rest under while you work. *A hot, stationary car is a deadly place to leave a child.*

Before your road trip or camping excursion into the desert, talk with your child about the importance of water intake and the need to drink frequently. Other than the signs of dehydration mentioned earlier, one behavioral change that I have observed in kids is an increase in crabbiness.

When hiking or camping, give your child some basic survival items and have them carry these at all times. At the minimum, a child should have:

• Whistle
• Water bottle(s)
• Salty snacks
• Garbage bag (instant shelter and more)
• Brimmed hat

Instruct your child to sit down and stay put if they become lost. This will allow searchers to locate them quicker and prevent them from wandering out of the search radius.

Lastly, practice some of the outdoor skills covered in this book so your child is more confident and comfortable in the outdoors. The desert is a place of wonder for kids if you provide them with the tools for safely exploring.

Stunning vistas await you.

OBTAINING WATER IN ARID REGIONS

If you spend enough time living in one place, you eventually begin to learn directly from the land. The land itself becomes the teacher. Books and formal courses are simply stepping-stones to understanding the academic side of nature. Strive for the trail wisdom of a native, which speaks of direct interaction with the natural world and carries with it volumes of *real* knowledge.

So it is with reading the landscape of the desert and locating water: you've got to think like a native not like a spectator or tourist. It's an awareness skill that can be a lifesaver.

In the chapter on Physiology, I discussed water requirements and methods for coping with heat stress. Here, I am going to cover methods for locating and collecting water.

If you don't have any water with you then conserve your own sweat. This means resting in the shade until the cooler hours of the evening, remaining clothed, and limiting your activity if possible. I'm talking about adapting— like the desert creatures do on a daily basis.

Again, I have to stress the single most important principle in this book: *Be prepared before you hit the trail.* For the dayhiker or motorist, the best approach to ensuring that your water needs are met is to use your faucet at home! Fill your water bottles and drink up before you walk out the front door. Also, pre-hydrate prior to your hike by filling that canteen known as your stomach.

When it comes to water sources in the backcountry, don't assume that the creek, spring, or creek you noticed on the map are going to even exist this year because it might not, especially during a season of drought.

On an extended backpacking trip, and certainly in a survival situation, it is important to know how to locate water for resupplying so let's look at some skills for procuring this precious substance.

Reading the Landscape

Being able to read the nuances of the land is a skill of visual acuity. You are searching for subtle clues written across the terrain that may indicate a spring, seep, or water hole. This is a skill that comes with experience hiking in the desert.

Precious Pockets of Water

A Word on Purifying Water

Parasites like Giardia can often be found in wilderness water sources throughout North America. Should you find yourself in a survival situation though and lack the means of purifying water (i.e., using a filter, adding iodine, or boiling for one minute) just keep in mind that waterborne illnesses can be cured. However, there is no cure for death from dehydration. The incubation period for Giardia is 1-3 weeks so it's not likely to affect you during a short-term survival episode. Drink up and go see your doctor after you are rescued. Don't risk dying of dehydration because the water is muddy or filled with algae. The saying in the survival field is: *Grit your teeth to strain out the big stuff!*

Seasonal cache of water in an Arizona Sycamore.

Places to Look for Water:
- Shady areas at the base of cliffs
- Rock pockets and depressions
- Tree cavities and hollows
- Undercut banks in dry riverbeds
- Where insect life abounds
- Where vegetation abounds: willow & cottonwood trees can sometimes have water at their bases.

Remember, a hike to a suspected water source is going to cost you physiologically, in terms of your own precious sweat, so make certain that you are headed *towards* water.

Tinajas
This is a Spanish word meaning *Earthen Jar*. Many people out west just call them *tanks,* as in water tanks. Essentially, tinajas are depressions in rock where water can be found by the gallons, if the rains have been good that year.

In tinajas in shaded overhangs, I have found water holes large enough to swim across. So important were these water sources that many times you can look around and find petroglyphs from the ancient peoples whose lives depended on these precious pockets of life. Water is considered sacred by native peoples where I live and understandably so since without it life would not be possible in so arid a land.

If you camp out near a tinaja or tank do so from a distance and be mindful not to wash your dishes, use soap, bathe, or otherwise contaminate these delicate, micro-worlds of life. For many animals, it may be the sole source of water for miles around.

Gathering Water
Sippy tubes
A handy item for the desert traveler to carry is a 3' piece of aquarium tubing. It can be used for extracting water from tiny seeps and crevices where your water bottle can't fit. It can also be used to skim water off the top of rain puddles.

Bandanna

With dozens of uses in the backcountry, no one should leave home without this little treasure. They are useful for mopping up water from rock pockets and for collecting dew early in the morning. A few of my students who were in the military stationed in desert regions, went a step further and carried small sponges in their survival kits for emergency dew collection.

Dew should be collected before sunrise (you may have only 20 minutes to gather it so move fast). Be careful not to gather from toxic plants such as poison ivy.

If you are by your vehicle, collect dew off the hood and surface making sure to avoid any chemicals or oil on the surface.

Your stomach can expand to hold one quart or more so fill up!

Ziplocs & Improvised Items

Ziploc baggies are mighty handy for getting back into rocky crags and crevices. Most of my first-aid items are secured in Ziplocs and I always throw in a few extras for water procurement.

Other than that, be resourceful. One woman, who was lost for several weeks in the Grand Canyon, used her eyeglass case to collect water from a tiny trickle seeping out of a rock. If you're stranded in the desert during the rainy season, spread out tarps, jackets, ponchos, and other objects to collect the rainwater. You may even find discarded pop and beer bottles that fill up with water that can then be purified.

Desert Survival Misconceptions About Water Sources
Water From a Barrel Cactus

The notion of slicing open a juicy barrel cactus and scooping out a cup of water to quench your thirst sounds appealing. The problem is that, due to the alkaloids present in the cactus, most people experience severe cramping and vomiting, which only increases their dehydration.

A refreshing drink from a barrel cactus? Think again!

Furthermore, the amount of moisture found in a barrel cactus depends on seasonal rainfall. Assuming that you have the tools (i.e., machete, tire-iron, etc...) to cut into the spiny cactus without injuring yourself, you have just killed a succulent that may be over one hundred years old not to mention protected by law.

Save the romantic notions for the Hollywood westerns and rely on this method only if there is no other alternative. By the way, the only barrel cactus that isn't toxic is the fishhook barrel (*Ferocactus wislizeni*).

A Pebble Under the Tongue

My father, who was in WWII, said he always kept a pebble under his tongue to help with the cottonmouth associated with long, hot marches. Psychologically, he said it helped. Remember, though, that this method only alleviates your dry throat and does nothing to fight dehydration since water is not being added to your system.

Collecting Water With a Solar Still

The solar still involves digging a two foot deep pit with a three foot diameter, placing a container in the bottom, and covering the whole pit with a six foot by six foot piece of clear plastic. The plastic condenses ground moisture on the interior covering where it funnels down to the center and drops into the container.

Constructing a still involves expending considerable amounts of your precious sweat to dig the pit. It also presupposes that you have a sheet of clear plastic and a shovel. If you had the foresight to bring this gear then you probably had the good sense to pack plenty of water.

The solar still just isn't that useful in the desert and yet it still shows up in survival books as a reliable water-collecting device. I have constructed many over the years in each of the four North American deserts. Each time I arrive at the same conclusion after seeing the results: *Plan ahead and carry plenty of water!* If you hadn't already guessed, this is the mantra that a desert explorer has to live by.

Water from a Tree Still

Transpiration bags or tree stills are a lot more efficient than solar stills, but not by much. Place a clear plastic bag on a leafy, non-toxic tree or patch of vegetation, tie the open end, and let it bake in the direct sunlight for the day. A rock in the bottom of the bag will weight it down so the fluid stays in.

A solar still and a transpiration bag sitting in direct sunlight.

When students use these during my desert survival classes, the amount of fluid obtained varies from a few tablespoons to one cup. Leafy trees like cottonwood and willow provide the most.

One observation I want to point out is that the liquid is distilled plant fluid and not fresh tap water. A cupful of *essence of cottonwood* is mighty strong in flavor and not very tasty. I have drunk (more like gagged down) liquid from tree stills but it was when I was hydrated and had a full stomach. Due to the bitter taste, I suspect that there would be the potential for vomiting to contend with, if this method were used in a true survival situation with accompanying dehydration. Worse yet, you could have an allergic reaction to such concentrated plant fluids. You can, however, use the liquid for pouring on your head or clothes to help keep cool.

Tree stills are a last-ditch method but one to consider in a waterless region, assuming you packed along some trash bags. Clear bags are required as black bags simply bake the vegetation.

Hazardous Sources to Avoid
Urine

Each summer, immigrants crossing from Mexico to Arizona across the desert are found carrying milk-jugs filled with their own urine in the hopes of extending their survival time. Urine, however, is a waste product and will only further dehydration because of the stress placed on the kidneys to process the toxins. People have used it for evaporative cooling by placing it on their clothes but you certainly don't want to drink it.

Radiator Fluid

Some older survival manuals used to recommend this as a source for obtaining drinking water. Perhaps decades ago, before antifreeze was introduced and the radiator was filled with straight tap water. Radiator coolant today is a deadly poison and not an option for drinking!

Poisonous Sources

In some regions of the West, you will find springs labeled on maps with titles like *Poison* or *Arsenic Springs*. They are named as such for a reason so respect the mapmakers. Arsenic can be found naturally in the water in some desert regions. Other springs might be contaminated with accumulated poison from the mining of uranium. These sources can be deadly. To know about specific water sources in the area where you're hiking, stop and ask the locals or call the Forest Service office for that region.

Avoid drinking from water that is devoid of any life!

Mineral-Laden Water

Sterile water may be contaminated or have a strong concentration of minerals present which, if consumed, will have you doubled over with severe cramps. Look for water that has algae, wrigglers, and pollywogs in it. There's a reason it is teeming with life.

The *Watered-Down Version* of How to Stay Hydrated

1. Remain in the shade.
2. Restrict activity to the cooler hours.
3. Monitor your urine color- clear is best.
4. Get off the hot ground- sit on your pack.
5. Remain clothed- remember the cowboy.
6. Work, if you have to, in increments- pace yourself.
7. Stay out of the wind.
8. Soak your shirt in water to aid with cooling.
9. Don't eat unless you have plenty of water to drink.
10. Ration your sweat not your water. Keep water in your stomach, not in your canteen.

DESERT SURVIVAL SHELTERS

Shelter in any region of the world comes down to one critical question—*how will you maintain your 98.6 degree body temperature in the environment that you are in?*

A shelter doesn't mean constructing a bark mansion, but rather providing for a roof over one's head. You probably won't have much to work with anyway given the sparse resources in desert regions. If the air temperature is hovering near 120 degrees, then constructing a shade shelter, remaining hydrated and clothed, and staying out of the wind are the key factors needed for survival.

During the cold winter months, where the nighttime temperature can plummet to 10 degrees or lower, you will need to make a fire and construct a more elaborate shelter to prevent hypothermia.

Shelter Types
Your Vehicle
During the hotter months of the year, your vehicle will become an *oven-on-wheels* and be too hot to reside in during the day. Instead, seek shelter in the shade of a rock outcropping, near some bushes, or even under your car if you can dig out a small depression without taxing your body's cooling mechanism. Remember to stay off the hot ground by sitting on a pack, spare tire, or extra clothes.

If your vehicle has removable seats, take one out and place it in the shade. A top-opening tailgate on a van or SUV can provide an instant shade source outside the vehicle.

At night, if it cools off, you can most likely return to your vehicle for some rest. In the colder months, if you have enough fuel to run your vehicle do so sparingly (15 minutes every hour to conserve fuel) and make absolutely certain to crack a window open to avoid carbon-monoxide poisoning.

The Versatile Tarp Shelter
Whether used for protection from the sun, wind, rain, or snow, an emergency blanket or tarp is an indispensable piece of survival gear.

If you have come prepared then this may be the only shelter you need

Tarp attached to truck (note duct tape on right corner).

Suspended shelter anchored by rocks and propped up with sticks.

to provide protection from the elements. Without a tarp you'll probably have to rely one of the primitive shelters that follow.

Caves

Rock ledges and caves provide ready-made shelters for getting out of the sun, wind, and cold. I have slept in many such shelters over the years out of necessity but try to avoid them if possible. I usually don't get a good night's rest in a cave due to the curious nature of mice and packrats who view me as part of their belongings. Such rodents can be a hazard since they might be potential carriers of the deadly hanta virus.

Caves can also have their share of insects, scorpions, and occasionally snakes. They are great for shade during the day but if you have to spend a night in a cave, sleep near the entrance rather than back in the recesses to avoid the critters.

Should you make a fire in a cave, be very careful where you build it. Rocks in the ceiling can dry out from the campfire's heat and drop on you! Try to place your fire just outside the lip of the cave to avoid this danger.

Thoroughly inspect the ceilings of ledges & caves for loose rocks.

Small wickiup constructed in one hour from dead branches & bark.

Wickiups

The shelter of choice for native cultures throughout the Southwest is the wickiup. The Navajo and Apache Indians still utilize this shelter design. The wickiup is a half-tipi that relies on three foundation poles for the frame. After the tripod is lashed in place, the spaces are filled in with additional poles and then covered with a layer of bark, shrubs, or debris. A thick layer of insulation on the floor provides protection from the heat (or cold) of the earth.

Underground Shelters

Excavated trench shelters are popular in the military where concealment is important. I have only used a handful of these over the years and don't like them because they invite a lot of critters inside and the walls tend to crumble gradually through body movement. They also require a digging implement and a fair amount of sweat to construct.

Still, if you have a tarp and are in a barren region without any natural shelter materials then this might be your only means of getting out of the elements. It's always good to have as many skills tucked under your belt as possible—*the more skills you possess, the more options you have.*

Subterranean shelter covered with a tarp.

The Coal Bed

For unparalleled warmth in cold weather, dig a pit the size of your torso and a foot deep then build a fire in it. After 4"– 6" of coals accumulate, cover the pit and coals with 2" or more of dirt. You now have an earthen heating pad to sleep on. This is an excellent, time-tested method and my personal favorite. Particularly useful in regions where wood for an all-night fire is lacking. This technique is illustrated in greater detail in *Practical Survival.*

A Bed in the Desert

Venture out on a moonlit night and you will discover the desert floor is alive with insects, spiders, scorpions, moths, and myriad creatures making their living during the cooler hours. A significant amount of the desert's biomass is composed of insect life. With that in mind, you will want to remember the following tips when sleeping out in the open.

- Use a walking stick to clear away any cowpies, debris, rocks, and wood in a 20' circle around your campsite to avoid scorpions and other insect pests.

- When collecting firewood or shelter materials, don't place your hands where you can't see.

- Be mindful that small, circular patches of open ground completely devoid of plant life could be an ant mound. This seems like common sense, but people occasionally think these are pre-cleared, inviting campsites. Fire ants will let you know otherwise! Similarly, areas near animal dens or piles of animal droppings should be avoided.

- Look out for environmental hazards such as loose rocks, dead standing cacti, cholla, and especially bee's nests.

- Never camp in a drainage or dry wash. Flash floods can sweep through these with deadly force.

FIREMAKING SKILLS

In a desert survival situation you will need fire—if not for warmth then for boiling water, cooking, signaling, keeping insects away, and companionship during a night alone. Get in the habit of carrying at least three firemaking sources on you. A lighter in your shirt pocket, waterproof matches in your pants pocket, and a magnesium spark-rod in your pack. Like any physical skill, firemaking is a perishable technique that must be practiced on a regular basis.

Firemaking Basics

The three elements for creating fire are: *Heat, Fuel, & Oxygen*. Heat refers, of course, to the flame produced by your lighter or matches, which is why you want to have several means of making fire with you at all times. Fuel is composed of tinder material such as bark or grass, followed by a layer of pencil thick twigs, and then finger-thick sticks. When constructing a fire, don't pack your structure of sticks and twigs too tightly because fire requires oxygen to burn.

Remember to clear away flammable debris within a ten-foot radius of your fire pit and always thoroughly soak your fire with copious amounts of water if you are going leave and not return. If there is a fierce wind blowing and danger of your fire getting out of control, then you may have to wait until the wind dies down before having one. *Exercise good judgment!*

Firemaking Tips

- An excellent technique for starting a fire when you are wet, cold, or need to signal for help immediately is to use a bundle of twigs. Gather a fist-sized bundle of fine twigs from a dead standing tree and stuff it with shredded bark or grass. Light the bundle off of the ground for maximum air exposure and then place it carefully in your fire pit.
- One of the best emergency fire starters is 100% cotton balls smeared with Vaseline. One of these will burn 4-5 minutes and a batch can be stored in a film canister. A 3' by 3' section of wax paper will also work but has a shorter burning time.

- Spark-based fires such as those made with a commercial sparking rod or a magnesium firestarter are superior methods of lighting a fire once you have mastered the skill. This method works particularly well with cotton balls.
- Starting a fire with optics such as a magnifying glass or binoculars requires the use of pithy plants or rotten wood to create a glowing ember. Then the ember is transferred to a bark tinder-bundle and blown into flame. Plant stalks like mullein, agave, yucca, or sunflower will create a good ember as well as dry animal scat from deer, cow, elk, and rabbits.

Collect fine twigs and then ignite the bundle off the ground.

- A woodless fire can be made in a barren environment using oil or transmission fluid from your vehicle, plane, or ATV. Fill a metal container with several handfuls of sand or dry dirt, and then pour in enough fluid to saturate the sand. Stir the entire mixture and light it. Avoid using gasoline due to the vapors.

- Sap from trees such as mesquite and pine is a superior material for igniting wet wood. Collect the honey-like resin from tree wounds and insert into your bundle of twigs. Sap will ignite even if it's wet.
- Keep your fire small and be conservative with fuel as most desert regions are lacking in firewood and you may have a long night ahead. You can dramatically decrease your fire's heat-loss by making a knee-high fireplace of piled rocks or dirt. Don't use rocks from a wash or riverbed as the moisture inside can cause a heated rock to violently explode!
- Bark scorpions are so named because they often cling to the under ides of dead wood. Use gloves or prod potential firewood with a stick but don't put your hands where you can't see.

Remember- always carry THREE sources of fire!

There are mysteries and wonders around each bend.

KNIFE USE AND SAFETY

Creating fire and making shelter along with countless other tasks will most likely entail the use of a knife at some point. Most of us today don't grow up utilizing a knife on a regular basis so it can become a dangerous tool in the hands of the untrained. By contrast, many of my cowboy friends teach their kids how to use a knife by the time they are five.

There are a couple of basic rules to keep in mind when carving and whittling. *This is nothing new*—just safety basics that every boy and girl scout learns.

- Never carve towards yourself.
- Always be aware when other people are sitting around you.
- Never stick your knife in a log or leave it lying on the ground. A knife belongs either in your hand or in its sheath.
- Get in the habit of keeping your elbows on your knees when carving to stay clear of the femoral artery in the leg as well as your groin area.
- When you start getting tired, that's the time to stop carving.
- Avoid folding knives. These can cause serious injury if the blade collapses on your fingers. Instead use a lockblade or a fixed-blade that has a tang running through the handle.

My preferred outdoor knife is the fixed-blade Swedish *Mora* knife that holds an edge like no other. I also carry a *Leatherman Wave* in my truck for vehicle repairs. *Victorinox* Swiss Army knives are also excellent and come in a wide array of models, including a lockblade version.

There are an endless variety of blades out there so shop around and find one that feels good in your hand and will meet your particular outdoor needs. A good knife is indispensable and a trusted friend in the backcountry. Carry one with you at all times.

Always carve away from yourself and stay clear of your vitals.

A Leatherman Wave & three versions of Mora blades.

SIGNALING FOR RESCUE

The ability to signal for help during a wilderness emergency is a critical skill. Like most survival techniques, you should practice this important skill before you actually have to use it.

Many people who are lost consider only a single method of attracting attention such as a smoky fire. There are dozens of methods, though, that can help draw attention to your whereabouts and the more you use the better your chances of rescue. Remember that to a searcher in a helicopter thousands of feet above, you are just a speck amidst a landscape of rocks and trees.

Here are some things to consider when signaling:

First, get into an opening or on a hilltop rather standing in a cluster of shrubs. Next, spread any items you can find in a twenty-foot circle around you. This is *passive* signaling. Then, look around and see what you have in your pockets, pack, or vehicle such as bright-colored clothing, ponchos, trash, jewelry, pop cans, etc... The idea is to increase your visibility so use anything you can find. You can even hang items in trees. After this you can work on active signaling using devices you have brought with you or improvised from nature.

Rescued in a Flash: The Amazing Signal Mirror

Perhaps the best method for attracting attention to yourself is through the use of a signal mirror. This is an excellent *active* signaling device and its glare can be seen from many miles depending on your location and weather conditions. The record for a survivor signaling with a mirror stands at 105 miles but the average range is between 30-60 miles on a clear day. The best signal mirrors are made of glass but plastic versions will work too. Either type will provide you with the means of having a shining moment in the wilderness.

To properly use a mirror, first make a V with your index and middle finger. This is your way of targeting the search plane or vehicle in the distance. With the signal mirror in the other hand, flash the reflection on to the palm of your opposite hand, just under the V. Slowly raise up the reflection on your palm so it goes up through the V of your fingers and you should then be making a direct flash.

Use a CD-Rom for practice and form a V to sight-in your target.

Practice this technique with a friend on your next hike or in your back-yard and you will be prepared in the event you ever end up in an emergency. Remember with signaling an overhead plane, that you may only have 1-3 minutes while the plane is in view so you need to have your signaling area and materials setup in advance.

When you spot the rescuers in the distance, start using your signal mirror, smoky fire, or flashlight (at night). Don't stop signaling until a rescuer puts his hand on your shoulder. As the saying goes, *it ain't over until it's over.*

A signal mirror can work at night as well, though with reduced performance. Doug Ritter, editor of the survival web-site *Equipped To Survive* (www.equipped.org), rigorously tests survival gear and has found in his fieldwork that a quality signal mirror can send a flash up to 3 miles on a bright, moonlit night.

Other Methods

Aside from using a mirror, you will have to look around at your immediate environment and improvise using rocks and debris. In an open field or clearing, you can spell out in large letters (20' long or more) the words HELP or SOS. Alternatively, you can spell out these words in the sand using a stick or laying down rocks.

Other items that can work are a cosmetic mirror, vehicle mirror, aluminum foil, bottoms of tin cans, chrome hubcaps, a whistle, car horn, and the shiny interior from a headlight or large flashlight. There are also commercial devices such as flares, laser lights, and strobe lights available at many outdoor gear shops that you can carry with in your pack along with a signal mirror.

A Shot in the Dark

A lady in a survival class of mine, who had been stranded atop a mountain on a winter night, used the flash from her disposable camera to alert a rescue team to her whereabouts! One search and rescue leader told me that he has even located lost hikers at night by using nightvision goggles to detect the light of cell phones, lighters, and illuminated wristwatches.

I tell my survival students to find at least five ways of alerting rescuers to your location using the above methods rather than relying on a single method. Make all of your resources, passive and active, work for you. *Remember that you have to take an active role in helping rescuers locate your position.*

Signal Fire

Using a smoky fire to signal for help is the method that often comes to mind with most people lost in the outdoors but its effectiveness is overrated. A signal fire can work but it must be used with caution.

If you decide to employ this method, please consider the following: 1) It needs to be a non-windy day to ensure that the billowing smoke will rise upward and not be dispersed. 2) You need to exercise caution in building a fire which means clearing the ground around your fire pit and making the fire in the open as opposed to in dense brush. 3) If your fire gets out of control and starts a range fire, you have not only endangered yourself and the fragile desert but also dozens, perhaps hundreds, of searchers who may be walking in your direction.

This very situation occurred in Arizona during the summer of 2002 and the recklessness of a single hiker decimated thousands of pristine acres of wilderness along with hundreds of homes.

When any of us ventures into the outdoors, we have a responsibility to ourselves, to the wilds, and ultimately to the rescuers who may put their own lives on the line trying to save us if we do become stranded.

As you may have guessed, I am not an advocate of signal fires. Many of the desert regions of the Southwest can boast of having 300+ days of sunshine a year so always carry a signal mirror. Rely on a signal fire only if the situation demands it or you have experience with this method.

Patterns of Three

A pattern of three is the universal code for distress. This means a series of three signals continually repeated from your whistle, car horn, mirror, camera flash, or shots in the air from your rifle.

It doesn't work too well with a bow & arrow, though!

Help searchers locate you by increasing your visibility.

SUMMARY

Throughout this book we have looked at some of the principles and skills involved in surviving in the desert. The theme, which runs through each chapter, is really about two words: *Planning and Preparation*. The most important thing to keep in mind is that survival isn't something that happens when things go terribly askew in the backcountry. Survival is an *attitude of awareness* that needs to occur before you leave your house for a trip into the wild places.

One of my anthropology professors, who spent considerable time living with the Australian Aborigines, used to say, "Anything that can happen in the desert will happen, and always at the least convenient time, so be prepared."

Remember to leave a travel plan with someone, carry basic survival gear (and Lots of water), and know your limits.

The latter point especially applies today as more people are venturing into the wilderness with the aid of GPS units, SAT phones, and SUVs. With such high-tech gear it's easy to be lulled into a false sense of security and to forgo using common sense.

Common sense has to do with utilizing the greatest survival tool you have: *your brain*. Use it on your outdoor trips and you will become an expert at the most important strategy of all- avoiding a survival situation.

Should you, however, find yourself lost, remember your survival is largely dependent on a positive outlook and your *will* to make it back alive. Adapt to your surroundings and conserve your energy until the cooler hours.

Beyond the physical skills and knowledge presented in this book there lies a deeper realm where the mind and soul can embrace the landscape as a place to live rather than to merely survive. This connection comes with time spent out in the wilds. As your experience grows, you may discover a shift from being a visitor to belonging to the land. Then you are truly at home in the desert.

Basic Survival Gear List for Dayhikers
- ❑ Lighter
- ❑ Magnesium spark-rod
- ❑ Matches in waterproof container
- ❑ Pocketknife
- ❑ 50' rope
- ❑ Space blanket or Emergency blanket
- ❑ Signal mirror
- ❑ Garbage bag
- ❑ Potable Aqua Iodine tablets
- ❑ Mini first-aid kit
- ❑ Salty snacks
- ❑ 2-6 quarts of water depending on the season
- ❑ Brimmed hat
- ❑ Sunscreen
- ❑ Appropriate clothing (long pants & long-sleeved shirt)

Essential Gear for Children
- ❑ Garbage bag
- ❑ Lighter*
- ❑ Pocketknife*
- ❑ Signal mirror *
- ❑ Salty snacks
- ❑ 2-6 quarts of water
- ❑ Whistle
- ❑ Brimmed hat
- ❑ Sunscreen
- ❑ Appropriate clothing for the season

*depending on age

Did you leave a travel plan with someone?

Do you have at least 2 gallons of water per person, per day in your vehicle?

Appendix

Suggested Reading and Resources

Books

A Natural History of the Sonoran Desert. Edited by Steven J Phillips and Patricia Wentworth Comus, Arizona-Sonora Desert Museum Press, Tucson, 2000.

Desert Survival Skills. Alloway, David. Austin: University of Texas Press, 2000.

Desert Survivor. Annerino, John, Four Walls Eight Windows, New York, 2001.

Life at the Extremes: The Science of Survival. Ashcroft, Frances. Flamingo, London, 2001.

Medicine for Mountaineering. Wilkerson, James A., The Mountaineers, 2001.

National Audubon Society Nature Guides: Deserts. MacMahon, James A., Knopf Publishers, 1997.

Over the Edge: Death in Grand Canyon. Gighlieri, Michael P. and Myers, Thomas M., Puma Press, Flagstaff, 2000.

Physiology of Man in the Desert. Adolph, E.F. and Associates, 1947.

Sierra Club Naturalist's Guide: The Deserts of the Southwest. Larson, Peggy, Sierra Club Books, 1977.

Wild Plants and Native Peoples of the Four Corners. Dunmire, William W. and Tierney, Gail D., Museum of New Mexico Press, 1997.

Periodicals

Backwoodsman Magazine, Charlie Richie, Editor/Publisher, Westcliffe, Colorado, 719/783-9028.

Bulletin of Primitive Technology, Dave Wescott, Editor, Rexburg, Idaho, 208/359-2400.

Wilder News, Newsletter of Wilderness Medical Associates, Bryant Pond, Maine, 207-665-2707, www.wildmed.com.

Wilderness Way Magazine, Kelly Lily, Publisher, Bellaire, Texas, 713/667-0128.

Survival Related Courses, Gear, and Outdoor Products

Ancient Pathways
Arizona-based wilderness skills company that offers 1-7 day courses on desert survival and bushcraft. Also carries signal mirrors, Mora knives, emergency blankets, and survival kits. Call 928/774-7522 or www.apathways.com.

Grand Canyon Field Institute
Offers 1-7 day courses on desert ecology and natural history as well as providing extensive backpacking trips in the Grand Canyon and throughout northern Arizona. Call 928/638-2485 or www.grandcanyon.org/fieldinstitute.

Recreational Equipment Incorporated (REI)
Nationwide outdoor retailer that carries a small line of survival products along with an extensive line of backpacks, tents, sleeping bags, clothing, and other outdoor gear. Maker of StormProof Matches. 1-800-426-4840 or REI.com.

Equipped to Survive
THE website for comprehensive survival gear reviews including information on survival kits, signaling, and techniques. Visit www.equipped.org.

*If you enjoyed this book then check out the
first one in the series:*

Practical Survival Tips, Tricks, & Skills
by Tony Nester

A hands-on manual for preparing for backcountry travel and handling wilderness survival situations throughout North America. Filled with detailed photos and field-expedient tips.

$8.95 plus $3 shipping
Available through Diamond Creek Press as well as
Amazon.com, and REI outdoor retail stores.

You can also order online at:
www.desertsurvivalskills.com
or call 1-928-774-7522

About the Author

Tony Nester has been teaching bushcraft and desert survival courses since 1989. His company Ancient Pathways provides survival training courses for the U.S. Military, National Park Service, the Grand Canyon Field Institute, and corporations throughout the Southwest. Tony has been featured on NBC News, the Discovery Channel and in Outside Magazine. He resides in Flagstaff, Arizona with his family.

For information on desert survival field courses, corporate training seminars, or lectures, contact:

Ancient Pathways, LLC
at www.desertsurvivalskills.com
or 928-774-7522